Talking about
Disability

Jillian Powell

RAINTREE
STECK-VAUGHN
PUBLISHERS
A Steck-Vaughn Company

Austin, Texas

Titles in the series

Talking about

Alcohol   **Disability**

Bullying   **Drugs**

Death   **Family Breakup**

© Copyright 1999, text, Steck-Vaughn Company

Published by Raintree Steck-Vaughn Publishers,
an imprint of Steck-Vaughn Company

Library of Congress Cataloging-in-Publication Data
Powell, Jillian.
Talking about disability / Jillian Powell.
       p.   cm.—(Talking about)
       Includes bibliographical references and index.
       Summary: Discusses disabilities, who has them, the physical and social challenges faced by disabled people, how they can work and play, and what kinds of help are available, with an emphasis on physical disabilities.
       ISBN 0-8172-5537-0
       1. Handicapped—Juvenile literature.
       1. Physically handicapped—Juvenile literature.
       [1. Physically handicapped.   2. Handicapped.]
       I. Title. II. Series: Powell, Jillian. Talking about.
       HV1568.P69   1999
       362.4—dc21   98-35438

Printed in Italy. Bound in the United States.
1 2 3 4 5 6 7 8 9 0 03 02 01 00 99

Picture acknowledgments
The publishers gratefully acknowledge the following for allowing their pictures to be reproduced in this book: Martyn F. Chillmaid, *cover, contents page*, 18, 19; Sally and Richard Greenhill 4, 5, 8, 9 (top), 10, 11, 12, 15, 22, 24, 25, 26, 27; A. Blackburn *title page* , 6; C.F.C.L/Image Select 7; Chris Schwarz 9; Impact/Peter Arkell 13 /John Coleman 14, 20 /Simon Shepherd 17, /Dave Young 23; Getty Images'/Jon Riley 16.

Contents

What is disability?

We are all different. We all have different abilities. There are things we can do, and there are things we can't do.

Disability means not being able to do
some things. When a person is disabled,
there are some things he or she cannot do.

Who is disabled?

One in ten people in the world is disabled. Sometimes you can tell that someone is disabled. Other times it is not so clear.

Disabled people are like everyone else.
They have their own ideas and feelings.
They have things they like doing.
But they have special needs.

Why are some people disabled?

Some people are born disabled. Some disabilities can be passed from parents to their children. Other people become disabled because of an illness or accident.

Some people become disabled when they get old. Other people are disabled for a while because they have hurt themselves in an accident.

What does physical disability mean?

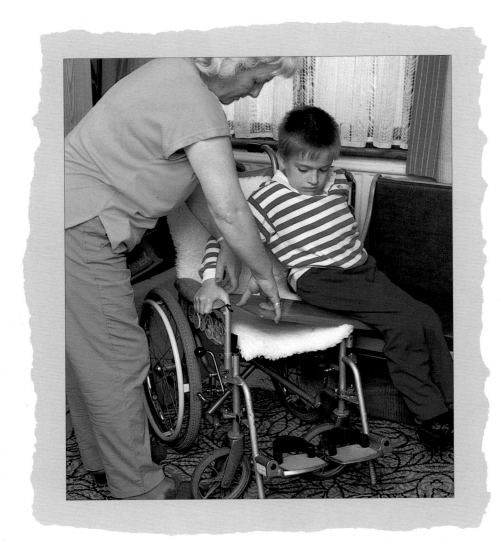

When someone is physically disabled, some parts of their body do not work very well. They may not be able to move parts of their body.

A person who is blind cannot see. A person who is totally deaf cannot hear at all.

Sally cannot hear very well. So she needs to wear a hearing aid.

How does it feel to be disabled?

People who are disabled have special needs. They may feel they have to try harder or work harder than others.

They want to try out lots of different things, to find out how many things they are able to do.

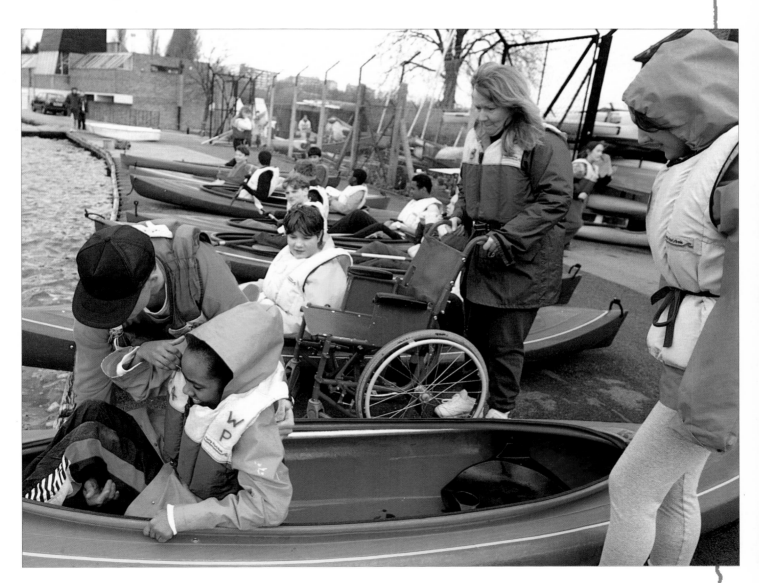

How can things be made easier for disabled people?

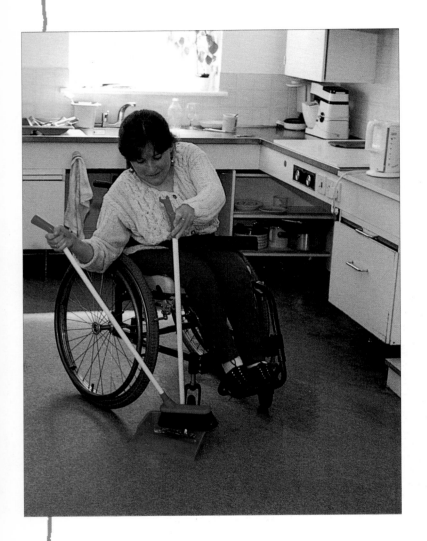

Some disabled people need wheelchairs to get around. They need to be able to move around and reach things easily.

Sometimes, changes need to be made to their homes to make everyday life easier for them.

People in wheelchairs can find it difficult to move around buildings that have stairs.

Elevators and ramps can make it easier to get around. Wide doorways help, too.

Can disabled people work?

Many disabled people are able to work. Like everyone else, they have different skills and abilities. But because of their special needs, it can sometimes be hard for a person with a disability to find a job.

This blind woman has a guide dog to help her get to and from work. Without her dog she would find it difficult to keep a job.

Can we do anything to help people who are disabled?

We should do our best to be friends with one another and help each other. It is wrong to treat disabled people differently from other people. It is also wrong to ignore people who are disabled or to call them names.

By spending time with people who are disabled, we can get to know them properly. We can find out what they think and feel about things.

Kirsty learned sign language so that she could talk to her friend Gita, who is deaf.

What other kinds of help are there for disabled people?

Science and technology have both helped to make life easier for everyone. Computers can help some disabled people and explain what they think or how they feel.

Some people who are blind use Braille to read. They learn to know words by touch.

Guide dogs help people who are blind get around safely.

These guide dogs will let their owners know when it is safe to cross the road.

Can people who are disabled enjoy sports?

People who are disabled can take part in many kinds of sports. They can enjoy water sports such as swimming and sailing. They can play team games such as wheelchair basketball or rugby.

People who are disabled can take part in sports competitions and races. Some sports have been designed especially for disabled people.

Wheelchair races are very popular.

Where can disabled people meet friends?

Like everyone else, people who are disabled can make friends at school. Or they can meet new people by joining clubs and groups.

Joe met a lot of new friends when he joined a youth group. Joe and his friends enjoy the same kind of music. They also like to play table tennis together.

How are disabled people special?

We are all different and we are all special.
We all have different things to give and
to share with each other.

Disabled people have special needs, but this does not keep them from enjoying life. Like everyone else, disabled people enjoy being themselves.

Notes for parents and teachers

Read this book with one child at a time or in groups. Ask them what kinds of disability they have heard about. Do they know anyone who is disabled?

Ask the children to close their eyes or cover their ears. Ask them how they feel and whether any of their other senses seem sharper.

Ask the children to think of something they do every day, such as a task or a journey. How easy would it be for someone in a wheelchair? What would need to be changed?

Talk about the way buildings can be changed to make things easier for people with disabilities. Include changes needed at home in rooms such as bathrooms and kitchens. Ask the children to think about any changes they would make at school to make things easier.

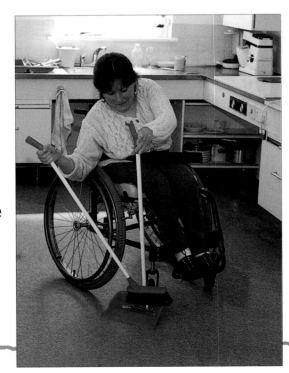

Disability charities or self-help groups may be willing to send someone to talk to the children. A talk on lip-reading and sign language could start a discussion about ways of communicating with each other when we cannot rely on words.

Ask the children what words they associate with someone who is disabled. It is important that they understand that name calling and using insulting words are unacceptable ways to behave.

Talk about the kinds of treatment that some people with disabilities need, for example, physiotherapy or kidney dialysis.

Talk about the kinds of disabilities people can have when they get older. Explain that in old age, some parts of our bodies can begin to wear out. Ask them if they know any old people who are disabled.

Talk about the Paralympic Games and some famous disabled achievers, in sports and other fields, such as Beethoven, Helen Keller, and Christy Brown.

Glossary

Abilities Things people are able to do.

Braille A kind of writing that uses raised dots so that blind people can read by touching.

Hearing aid Something worn by deaf people to help them hear.

Sign language A way of talking to people by making signs with your hands.

Skills Things people are good at doing.

Special needs Extra help that some people need.

Books to Read

Kent, Deborah. *The Disability Rights Movement* (Cornerstones of Freedom). Danbury, CT: Children's Press, 1996.

Landau, Elaine. *Blindness* (Understanding Illness). New York: 21st Century Books, 1995.

——. *Deafness* (Understanding Illness). New York: 21st Century Books, 1995.

Morrison, Jaydene and Lawrence Clayton. *Coping with a Learning Disability* (Coping). New York: Rosen Publishing Group, 1995.

Ratto, Linda L. *Coping with Being Physically Challenged* (Coping). New York: Rosen Publishing Group, 1991.

Sanford, Doris E. *Yes, I Can: Challenging Cerebral Palsy* (Children of Courage). Sisters, OR: Muitnomah Publishers, 1992.

Index

Numbers in **bold** refer to pictures as well as text.

DATE